Tales from the Teacup Palace

Karen Friedland

Červená Barva Press
Somerville, Massachusetts

Červená Barva Press
P.O. Box 440357
W. Somerville, MA 02144-3222

www.cervenabarvapress.com

Bookstore: www.thelostbookshelf.com

Cover Art: "Painting of Ham Green House" by Sarah Ann Bright (date unknown)

Cover Design: William J. Kelle

ISBN: 978-1-950063-42-0

ACKNOWLEDGMENTS

I would like to thank my husband Rich and my friends far and wide, online and off, for their support and encouragement, especially Renuka Raghavan and the fabulous Gloria Mindock.

I'd also like to thank the editors of the journals in which the following poems first appeared:

Nixes Mate Books: "Winter Light" Broadside, 2019

The Muddy River Poetry Review: "Angel Eyes"

Constellations: A Journal of Poetry and Fiction: "The Lost Song"

The Lily Poetry Review: "Life as a Faded Photograph"

Writing in a Woman's Voice: "Seven-Year-Old Girls' Sleepover Party, 1970" and "To the Trees"

Vox Populi: "Ridiculously Alive" and "Windows Are Open"

The Red Eft Review: "Marks"

First Literary Review East: "Having Built for Ourselves a House That Does Not Leak"

The Rye Whiskey Review: "Bad Tattoo" and "The Sadness of Used Jewelry"

TABLE OF CONTENTS

For Rich, the fur-kids, the Poetry Sisters, and Mr. Olson,
who built our house in 1930

Tales from the Teacup Palace

Having Built for Ourselves a House That Does Not Leak

in the pouring rain is the main thing—
having cobbled together
a bittersweet, New England
kind of life

amidst leaning gravestones
and old houses
with teacup-sized yards.

Years pass,
and you learn to survive the seasons
and the coldness.

But oh, the nearness of the ocean
and the blueness of northern skies!

Marks

It takes many years
for fingerprints to form
in odd places around the house—

where your husband clutches
at the newel post, say,
on his way down the stairs.

But the marks suddenly appear one sunny day—
above light switches and around door knobs and frames,
so you scrub the years-worth of dead skin and newspaper
ink away,

knowing all the while they're a talisman—
a sign of us having been here, in this house,
of having lived at all.

I look forward,
years from now,
to having the pleasure
of scrubbing them away again.

Winter Light

Scaling back, under cover,
waiting for spring to arrive:

these dogs, laying abed in the raw sun,
those bare trees, shaking outside the window
this chill day,

that frail human connection—
with a neighbor,
with words on a screen, on a page

are the lightest of filaments
that connect us,
that make us,
that save us.

Angel Eyes

Her name was Mary,
as a Catholic girl from West Roxbury
ought to be named,

but she moved to Colorado
and came back as "Angel"
and took up with Johnny,
the Vietnam vet with a drinking problem,
who grew up across the street.

She was only in her 50s
when she died of a fast-moving cancer,
having moved back in with her mother around the corner,
who was failing, too,
but outlived her.

Once, when things were still good,
Angel and Johnny showed up in fringed, black,
leather motorcycle gear,
proud,
to tell us they were going up to New Hampshire for the
weekend.

Before she died,
Angel had cards made up,
fashioning herself a dog-walker named "Angel-Eyes,"
though she rarely walked her own tiny Yorkie,
whose name now escapes me,
as so many things do.

She was just one
of my neighbors who died.

I went to her funeral Mass,

where her so-called normal relatives shook their heads
sadly
and scoffed.
"Her real name was Mary,"
they said.

The Lost Song

It was about love,
but I can never remember the lyrics,
or the melody, for that matter.

It was on the radio briefly,
during a difficult time
of love and death.

It was wispy,
ineffably lovely,
not well-known.

Someday, if I really apply myself,
I may find this lost song,
and the mysteries of the universe
will finally fall into place.

Bad Tattoo

Don't talk to your tattooist
about suicide
while she's injecting jet black ink
into the fragile, aging skin
of your upper back—

she will get distressed
and drill too deep,
leaving you with a permanent reminder—

a painfully-scarred tattoo
that will wake you up some nights,

making you wonder why you went this route,
at this late date,
of trying to send a mostly-hidden message
to the world—

Was it love,
Was it fear,
Was it middle-aged wanting?

At any rate, you weren't expecting pain,
but there you have it.

Life as a Faded Photograph from the 1970s

"Go wait for Daddy," our mother would say—
on the front concrete steps
before the trees grew big,
before the walkway turned into tasteful slate.

So we waited for Daddy
in the hazy, '70s sunshine,
in the hideously-patterned clothing of the day.

It was a ruse to get rid of us,
as it turned out—
but still we waited, Zen-like,
as if trapped in amber,
for what might've been hours.

Only to re-appear years later
as a faded yellow and green photograph,
when a certain song comes on the radio.

Mourning Doves Make the Best Music

Can I tell you how happy I am
with this humble little life?

With the paths I walk every day
with my dogs,
and the trees I know like lovers,
that bend in the wind.

Having finally learned
to fight nothing—

to let the world wash through me,
and simply be suspended
in the still blue sky
of an ordinary day.

Compose Rudimentary Praise Songs Daily

To the wind,
to the ever-changing weather,
to the birds that wake you,
to the city that bears you,
to the strange times
you happen to live in.

To your particular allotment of years—
your decades, your century—
to the music, words and famous people
who live there.

To the odd assortment of friends
whose paths you've haphazardly crossed
in the places where you landed,
as if pre-ordained.

But nothing is in fact pre-ordained—
it's all just happenstance magic.

Abject Braless-ness

Poor Dad—
the fad in Brooklyn that summer
was young women wearing the flimsiest of tank tops and
no bra,
and I was one of them.

Poor Dad had to pretend
that I didn't have my small breasts on full display
like a dessert tray, in that silly orange tank top.

Poor Dad—
always bringing up the rear of the party,
large camera bouncing jauntily on his chest
as we strode through rough city neighborhoods
on the edge of gentrification.

(Dad called it "the ghetto,"
to my sister's abject horror,
a big, mid-western smile
always on his upturned face.)

Now that you're gone, Dad
I'm sorry for all that we did and didn't do—
and I hope you knew that we loved you,
despite our indignant mortification
and abject braless-ness.

To the Trees

Mainly, I like your leaves,
and the knowledge that your roots
are everywhere—

burrowing deep through every square inch of soil,
seeking sustenance,
and chatting, apparently, with other beings.

So I let the blow-ins grow,
and now they're towering,
seeking out the sun
and flowering,

providing us with infinite beauty,
protecting us
from the pitilessness of over-exposure.

The Poetry Reading

The seriously-published poet
goes on just a little too long,
and we collectively lose faith
in her vaunted words,
her '70s, New York-style ennui.

She, in turn,
feels us slipping away like the tide,
less transfixed by the minute
by the torrent of honed words
that had so recently cossetted us.

So she picks up her tempo,
and we rustle uncomfortably in our seats

craving our own worlds,
craving release.

Replaced

Even the objects you thought you loved
eventually get replaced—
get worn down from years of use—
get old, tired, spent, frayed.

People at workplaces, too,
get replaced—
they flame out, move on,
go away.

Only the ghost of their forgotten names
on old documents, in old paper files
for a time remains—

So little to be remembered by.

Seven-Year-Old Girls' Sleepover Party, 1970

We went tribal, that night.
It was epic—
Near-naked, we painted flowers around our belly buttons
with a mother's lipstick

and formed warring camps—
fighting pitched hula-dance battles
until a mother came in,
pleading for mercy,
claiming 2 a.m.

And where, oh where, are those pleasure-drunk,
dancing seven-year-old wild girls now?

Old, with sagging bellies, I imagine—
frayed,
having been slit open repeatedly
to remove wombs, tumors, babies.

Yet, might we be yearning to break free,
paint flowers around our aging, wrinkled belly buttons
with lipstick, and fight pitched hula battles once more?

We might be.

To the Ant Man

at the commuter rail stop
in summertime,
who for years casually killed and maimed dozens of big,
black ants
daily with his rolled-up newspaper:

How could you do this
every single day
to such harmless beings,
merely trying to lead their lives?

To myself:
Why didn't you say a word to stop him?

Instead,
I watched closely as the maimed ants
silently thrashed about, trying to drag their writhing,
hopeless, half-alive selves away.

I felt sorrow.
I seethed inwardly.
I did nothing.

Now, I am ashamed.

Memorial Day

Old houses pop and crack
in the hot sun;
my dogs pant on our slow walk
past neighbors on shaded porches.

Out of nowhere, the wind rushes,
forming eddies in the trees—

and suddenly, my neighbors look old and gray—
because, suddenly, we *are* old and gray.

And time has warped itself
through me again:
the wisdom is in the trees.

Ridiculously Alive

I am thinking about
the small spaces I inhabit
and the tiny things
I see every day—the very stones on the road.

I am thinking
that I will continue to reject
that which insults my soul—
this gets easier every year.

I am turning my mind instead
to everything that is now living—
my husband on the couch, reading the paper,
the dogs, softly snoring beside us,
the late summer crickets, with their fading serenade.

Everything, I know, dies
but this does not grieve me right now—

Because at this moment,
everything is so brilliantly,
almost ridiculously, alive.

Done

All the hammering of the day is done—
by the men up on rooftops,
by the ones spreading asphalt,
by those installing raw wood fencing—

they can all head home, now,
covered as they are in sweat and grime,

while we walk our dogs silently at dusk
through a neighborhood prettified, subdued
and kept from rotting and sinking
back to the earth

for a time.

The Sadness of Used Jewelry

That bracelet you bought super-cheap off eBay,
that came from some podunk town in Mississippi,
that stinks of cigarettes
and the insides of some sad old dame's
hopeless purse—

You had hoped against hope,
it might be a treasure—
a shard of the world's beauty
with which to adorn yourself.

But let's face it—
you're low in income and middle-aged—

a truth no amount of airing out on the sun porch,
no amount of useless, cheap frippery
will ever disguise.

Surprise!

Eros and the Arts

Laying here, with my dogs,
I am day-dreaming about saucy male poets
who still know how to flirt—
a rare pleasure
in this blue, Calvinistic city of ours.

And I am fetched to higher realms,
such as where good poetry takes me—
because eros and the arts
are my main forms of transportation

in this humble little glimpse
of the world we are given.

Whose Boy?

Whose lanky boy is that,
walking awkwardly, endearingly, down the street?
He is our lanky boy.

Whose towering maple is that,
Half-dead, half majestically alive?
Again—ours, our street's.

Whose are these sauntering cats,
these aggrievedly-barking dogs, this late-summer,
almost-fall afternoon
that tastes like honey?

They belong to all of us—
this whole, wondrous slice of existence,

so lush,
this scene should be rendered in oil
on a vast canvas
as a testament to living.

In Which I Give Thanks

Thanks to the grueling hours I spend working for others,
I am able to buy for myself small things of beauty—
hand-painted plates, little ceramic birds and the like.

I am able to house
several heavily-breathing animals,
to feed them.

I am able to make dinner for us both,
and have it on the table nightly
for which, like Father Clancy,
I ought to give audible thanks:

So, for these plants
that gave their lives
to sustain us, thank you!
Amen.

Windows Are Open

Windows are wide open—
to the trees, to the birds,
to the day

Only this world,
Only to praise it.

Tunneling deep
into my own exhaustion,
I find I can barely lift a pen.

Mr. Crow
cleaves in half
this day,
and a small dog slumbers
against my back.

There's something to be said
for loving your life,
exactly as it is—

these dogs,
these songs,
this summertime.

Benediction, with Flowering Trees in Springtime

May your house
have windows onto flowering trees
and pictures on every wall.

May your house
be filled with loved beings
in good health
and benevolence in all their hearts.

May quietude,
mixed with bird song,
reign in your house.

May your soul
finally have found a home here.

ABOUT THE AUTHOR

A nonprofit grant writer by day, Karen's poems have been published in *Writing in a Woman's Voice*, *Nixes Mate Review*, *Vox Populi*, *The Lily Poetry Review, Constellations*, and others. Her previous book, *Places That Are Gone*, was published in 2019 by Nixes Mate Books. She lives in Boston with her husband, two dogs, two cats, and a few too many plants.

www.ingramcontent.com/pod-product-compliance
Lightning Source LLC
Chambersburg PA
CBHW020956030426
42339CB00005B/132